Saying thank you to God

by KAREN HOLFORD

*Dedicated to our Father God
who has given us so many things.
Thank you, God.*

First published in 2009
Copyright © 2009 Autumn House Publishing (Europe) Ltd.

Illustrations by Gustavo Mazali

All rights reserved. No part of this publication
may be reproduced in any form without
prior permission from the publisher.
British Library Cataloguing in Publication Data.
A catalogue record for this book is
available from the British Library.

ISBN 978-1-906381-42-4

Published by
Autumn House,
Alma Park, Grantham, Lincs.

Printed in Thailand

Autumn House

Preface

Giving our tithes and offerings back to God is an important part of our worship and Christian devotion. Children can understand about giving tithes and offerings, in a simple way, from a young age. The sooner children begin to understand that everything belongs to God and he shares it with us, the more natural it is to respond generously to God. This simple story is one way of helping children to understand what it means to pay our tithes and offerings. It aims to help your child understand that we give our tithes and offerings because we love God, and the act of giving money back to God is an act of thankfulness, appreciation and love.

After the story there are some extra ideas
for families and churches to use to help children
understand more about being good stewards of God's money.

Hannah was drawing a picture of her garden. She had coloured in the grass with her green crayons, and made a path by drawing some round, brown stones. Now she was hunting through her crayons for purples and pinks to draw lots of flowers around the edge.

Mummy came into the room carrying a package and some letters. 'Hannah! Look! I think Grandma has sent you a present!' Hannah dropped the purple crayon and slid down off her chair. The parcel was wrapped up in brown paper, and her name was written on the front in big, black letters. Grandma had stuck a big smiley face sticker on the back.

'Wow! A present from Grandma! Can I open it now?' Hannah began to pull at the sticky tape around the package.

Mummy laughed. 'All right then! You've almost opened it already!' The tape pulled off in one long piece and Hannah turned the package upside down and shook it gently.

Out fell something soft and bumpy, wrapped in tissue paper, and a letter from Grandma. Hannah tore open the tissue to find a funny-looking teddy bear with a flat tummy and no legs.

'Oh, look!' said Mummy, 'It's a puppet! Grandma has sent you a bear puppet. Try it on your hand.' Hannah put the bear puppet on her hand. She made the bear clap his hands and rub his nose. Mummy pretended to tickle the bear's tummy and Hannah made him laugh.

Hannah picked up Grandma's letter. 'Dear Hannah, here is a puppet for you to play with. You can give him a name and tell him all kinds of stories. Maybe next time I come he will sing to me and make me laugh! I hope you have lots of fun with him.
Love from Grandma x x x'

'Mmm,' said Hannah, 'I think I'll call him Tickle Bear.'

Hannah played with Tickle Bear. She made him sing a funny song and do all the actions. She even made Tickle Bear tickle Mummy's tummy too!

'I need to write and say thank you to Grandma,' said Hannah. 'I'll have to tell her he's called "Tickle Bear". I think that will make her laugh!' Mummy helped Hannah to write the letter. Hannah remembered her garden picture. 'Can I send Grandma my garden picture, too?'

'Yes,' smiled Mummy, 'that's a lovely idea.'

Hannah picked up a yellow crayon and drew a sun in the sky, and then some blue flowers. She turned the picture over and wrote, 'To Grandma, I love you, from Hannah x x x'. After they posted the letter and picture to Grandma, Hannah made Tickle Bear go to sleep. She even made him snore!

Mummy was busy at the table with piles of papers. 'What are you doing, Mummy?' asked Hannah.

'I'm adding up our money so I can give some back to God,' said Mummy.

'Why do you have to give some back?' asked Hannah, 'Can't we keep it all?'

'Well, it all belongs to God really, and he shares it with us. We give him back a little tiny bit, to say "thank you" for the big bit we keep. For every ten pounds God gives us, we give one back to God. You can help me count.' Mummy and Hannah counted the pound coins, and, when they got to ten, Hannah put one coin in a basket and they began to count all over again.

'Now what do we do? We can't post the money to God like we sent a letter to Grandma!' Hannah frowned.

'We put the money in a special envelope, called a tithe envelope, and take it to church.' Mummy gave Hannah the tithe envelope and Hannah put all the money inside. 'Tithe is an old word that means a tenth of something. Some of this money goes to pay people like Pastor Jake. They work for God, so the money is used to help them,' explained Mummy.

It was hard for Hannah to understand. So Mummy tried to help. 'It's like when you wrote to Grandma. You sent the letter to say "thank you" to Grandma. But you also sent her your picture to say "I love you". The tithe money is like saying "thank you" to God for letting us keep the rest of his money. The offering money is an extra gift. We give that to God to say we love him.'

'I want to say "thank you" and "I love you" to God, too!' Hannah found her purse. There was some money in the purse that Grandpa had given to her. She counted, 'One, two, three, four, five, six, seven, eight, nine, ten! Ten pounds! One pound is to say "thank you", and . . . how many pounds say "I love you"?'

'Whatever you want to give,' said Mummy. Hannah thought about all the things God had given her. A warm and safe house, toys, good food, a family who loved her and a Grandma and Grandpa who did so many fun things to make her happy. 'This time I want to give God five pounds to say I love him, because I love him very much!'

Mummy gave Hannah two white envelopes. She helped Hannah write 'Thank you, God' on her tithe envelope and 'I love you, God' on her offering envelope. Hannah wrote her name on the envelopes, too, just so God would know who they came from, and she drew pictures on the envelopes to make them look pretty.

Hannah took Tickle Bear to church. She put him in her bag with her two special envelopes. When it was time to collect the money, Tickle Bear picked up the two envelopes in his furry paws, and put them on the offering plate. After all, Tickle Bear had helped her to learn how to say 'thank you' and 'I love you' to God. Hannah looked at Tickle Bear and grinned. She tickled his tummy and made him laugh. 'Thank you, Tickle Bear,' she whispered in his ear, 'I love you, too!'

Ideas for families and churches:

- Children love to follow their parents' example. When parents pay their tithe and offerings with cheerfulness and generosity, the children will learn to do so, too.

- As a family, make sure that you spend time together talking about all the ways God has shown his love for you and blessed you. Involve your children in naming your blessings, drawing pictures of them in a scrapbook, writing a list of them, or collecting little items in a basket that remind you of all the good things God has given you. These will help the children to see how much they have to thank God for.

- Give your child two plastic cups or decorated jars and write 'Thank you, God' on one, and 'I love you, God' on another. Help them to count out their money into the different cups, and to choose how much they put in their 'I love you, God' cup.

- Children can be given wrapping paper and sticky tape so that they can wrap up their offerings as presents for God. Alternatively, provide them with white envelopes and crayons or felt pens. Then they can design and decorate their own tithe and offering envelopes, just as Hannah did. Try taking up the offering in a different way at your church occasionally. Let the children come to the front and put their money in a special gift bag or box, or in an unusual container. Perhaps they can pin their offering envelopes on a large heart-shaped pin board covered in red fabric, as a love gift to God, or stick their tithe envelopes to a large home-made 'Thank you' card, using putty adhesive or double-sided sticky tape.

 You might like to choose a special children's charity as a family and collect money to support its work. Your children can help raise money and visit the charity premises, or watch a video of its work, so they can see how their money is used to help others in very practical ways that they can understand.

 Teach children how to take care of their environment by recycling waste materials, sharing, giving unwanted toys or outgrown, good quality clothing to special projects, and respecting the resources they have.

 Make economy a fun game. Find interesting ways to save money by being willing to buy second-hand goods, make home-made gifts and cards occasionally, or set limits on the amount of money spent on gifts.

 Buy some items from environmentally-friendly and fairly-traded sources, and teach your children why it is important to spend money ethically where possible, even though it may be a little more expensive, because taking care of the Earth and other people are also ways of saying 'I love you' to God.

 Help children to save money for special items, rather than spending money as soon as they have it. Knowing how to save and being able to wait for the things they want are good skills for children to develop. Start with smaller projects that can be saved for in a month or so, and build up to bigger savings projects as they grow older.